ANN

RANDOM THOUGHTS

ON A LIFE, WELL, LIVED,
F NOT ALWAYS SO WELL-LIVED

outskirts
press

ODE TO POETRY

Where have you been all my life?
hidden in weary words,
soon to be thrown away?
Misunderstood as archaic angst,
cloistered by fear and shame?

Surely I am not good enough
for such a handsome fellow.
Yet you cosset me and comfort me
in countless ways I cannot
number nor express.

Until I take my pen and place,
a student at your feet,
hungry for a metaphor,
for smooth and soothing words,
ready to write and adore.

TABLE OF CONTENTS

RANDOM THOUGHTS
ABOUT NATURE

I AM A POET

I am a poet too small,
too inept and dull to express
the grandeur of the universe.
Yet I feel it with my poet's soul,
the width and breadth and wonder.
I can but stumble
from one delight to another,
grateful for its surprising beauty.

THE WORLD IS MY THERAPIST

The world is my therapist, I shall not care
if you cancel our appointment.
Every rock, tree, and flower,
every copse is a priestly bower.

My aura is a cloud of butterflies,
as I confess my sins to the evening breeze.
A choir hears my yearning in the setting sun,
when I complain of my neighbor's dis-ease.

Now you're sick and not ready, you say,
to hear confession, we must postpone
to another time and day.
Pshaw! I care not, I am not needy.

I will shout out my secrets loud and clear
for every soul in the universe to hear.
All I need is right here
in the beauty of the world's creation.

THE BEST OF THESE

I love the hills, the rocks and rills,
the flowers and fruits and fancy ferns.
I love all of nature, it seems,
except for roaches and rats,
spiders, snakes, and sardines.

But the best of these is trees.

I love the mountains,
the great white cliffs,
the sparkling streams, the vast open sea,
the quirky deep ocean things
with weird and wacky elbows and knees.

But the best of these is trees.

I love the little things,
the flowers that beckon from the forest floor,
the magnificent mauve of a maple leaf
in late fall, the poignant scent
of a fallen pine cone,
'neath the sturdy stone stile.

But the best of these is trees.

I love the immense blue sky
even more when it isn't blue,
but covered with scuddering clouds
that rush by neon orange streaks
from the setting sun.

But the best of these is trees.

MOTHER NATURE

We thought it was over.
Mother would use everything
to fulfill her worst tantrums.
Tornadoes, earthquakes, floods and fires,
everything naughty and nasty,
all of it to make us cry "uncle"
a TKO in the ring.

How many times did we wound her?
Like cancer it spread for years.
Oil spills, chemicals in the ocean,
pollution in the air,
Mother Nature was dying,
but did anyone care?
Only a few heard her death rattle
as the grim reaper came by.

Then she seemed to rally.
One more weapon she'd use.
The Corona Virus, the worst for us,
but for her, it's working, they say.
Clear skies, birds singing, water, deep and clear.
Can't we call a truce to end our ways
of self-inflicted madness and fear?

YOU COULD SAY

You could say I'm in the dusk of life,
the rosy, husky crust of life,
the time when pastel orange
merges with a pasteller aqua
and a bluish pink fills
the bowl of sky.

When my little dogs
take me for a walk of sorts,
to say hello to every tree,
and to human neighbors,
not as well loved, perhaps,
as you and me.

Then I might think of a vodka tonic.
Remembering the smoky haze of it
seems like a craving of sorts. But
when I return home, I've forgotten
the urge, needing only water,
and a bit of supper.

My elixir is the sky itself.
It satisfies my itch for beauty.

RANDOM THOUGHTS
ABOUT MUSIC

MUSIC

The person who sings
prays twice, I'm told.
But it's more than that, for me.
The mouth prays, the eyes weep,
the ear drums quiver and quake,
the music of my heart is
food for life, for me.

There have been times when
bankruptcies and betrayals
fell like prairie hailstorms.
When I was unloved and unlovable,
when I could not love even myself,
because of the hatred and hopeless hurting
until, until, I was redeemed by singing.

It seemed I would not survive
without Thursday's choir practice.
Even with disharmonies
and dis-rhythmic beats of Rock.
Even when we're asked to sing
strange sounds, from strange lands,
and even stranger composers.

Even when we struggle with
new notes of untuneful shape, with
scratchy sounds and coughing screeches
from flu-infested sopranos.
Even when the altos fight for control,
we can but wait and hope. Surely
it will be better soon.

Even if the conductor is clueless,
the singing cleanses and redeems. Even
if the singers are untalented and unschooled,
each throat warbles, each diaphragm heaves,
all the moving parts of our communal lungs
join in joyful jubilation.
Magic happens.

Our voices become ten,
then a hundred, with a good blend.
Yes, there's more in teamwork,
having sung a solo or two, I know.
When all the sounds mesh and merge,
making their way to the heart
and soul.

We must not forget that wizened thing
that waffles and wallows in wonder at times.
The soul becomes goose-bumpy,
with artful awe,
in many minds and megaphones.
All share a desire to move,
to motivate the one who hears.

Yet the poor listener cannot know
what we are feeling. Theirs is but
a poor substitute, sitting in that pew or chair.
Their ears may be swept away by beauty,
their eyes feast upon our effort, but
they can never feel the guts and gusto
of our play.

Once in a while,
in a special time,
a special place,
with a special piece,
when heads and hearts are one,
the conductor reaches in to play upon
our very soul.

No training teaches this, but
it is a special person indeed
who can power the baton
to be a force no one can disobey.
Can you imagine how that power
can be wielded and magnified
when love is at play?

Can you imagine if every soul
is offered up to be voiced
like the harps of Heaven?
No mistakes or unseemly chords,
because God herself has reached down
to craft the sound.

Then, oh then,
we are at peace,
healed and whole.
We are home.

ALL SAINTS SUNDAY

(after a performance of *Requiem for the Living* by Dan Forest, 2019)

A lone dove soars out of the silence.
A violin on its highest string whispers
like the thin stream of a light beam,
seeping into a dark universe.

More sounds out of nowhere,
giving substance to the firmament,
as cassocks and censors sway
a grim march down the hushed aisle.

Then the voices,
scarcely heard at first,
aching with reverence,
in awe of the holy moment.

Requiem Eterna, they sing,
calling forth memories of past loves
and the insatiable grief
of a million souls lost.

But they are not lost,
the voices sing.
A change of key and a lift
to the rafters above.

Holy! Holy! Holy!
Hosanna in the Highest!
The joy is profound as the sounds abound
and stir our deepest emotion.

Hearts are cracked open.
Tears flow. There is joy!
There is hope!
There is love!

As the music slows and grows quiet,
the parade of robes vanishes,
leaving the lone dove
to finish its flight.

Silence reigns again,
but we are changed.
We are blessed.
We are One.

RANDOM THOUGHTS
AROUND THE
NEIGHBORHOOD

OUR SMALL WORLD

I am no Mary Oliver,
though I might wish I were.
I don't know the names of things.
I live in a suburb, no Blackwater world
to enchant and inspire. Most of the time,
my poetic skills are lacking,
however much I try.

But when I walk with the dogs,
I talk to the trees. I share my thoughts
with what comes adrift
on the evening breeze.

The three Magnolias seem bewildered today.
No bloom yet? They're dry and browning.
"What do you lack," I say, "but the rain
which was wild and whimsical this winter?"

I like to touch the crooked tree
and rejoice a bit. Struck by lightning,
it is clad again in gaudy, green leaves,
proving resilience and love of life.

And the flowers!
So many beauties this year.
The blue Iris in Norma's yard
asks about my mood and
the red and white Clivia
complains of the cold
by the Myers' fence.

On the corner, ten-foot high Hollyhocks,
in red, white, and pink, are having an argument.
High and haughty, they ignore the resting roses
and geraniums of the same hue.

Mountain Hawthorne and Tulips of yellow
greet me with a smile. And that blue stuff spilling
over the walk, like the owner who glares from
the window, watches, to make sure I pick up the poop.

But the busy birds! They hold a convention
every night at dusk, holding forth on the gossip
of the day, talking all at once as if to say
Hear me! My news is best today!

Chattering like Quaker professors
who argue to reach a consensus.
Would that all people would do as well,
swallowing politics and faiths with a chirrup.

ONLY HIM CAN DO THAT

Only Him can do that,
my neighbor said.
The sunset was swallowed
in a baby blue sky,
neon yellow, orange and red.

She often comes round to greet me,
as I walk by with my three dogs.
You see the doc? She asks
as they lash and thrash on their leash.

We share a cancer diagnosis
and an abdominal surgeon.
(Or should I say abominable?
Mine was a false alarm.)

Strange that we are close, neighbors that care,
despite the language, sharing many ways.
I think it must be true:
Only Him can do that.

When I find a new flower
or a languid Durufle tune,
It bubbles up – this joy.
Only Him can do that.
It comes when we visit an old tree,
scarred by a lightning spree
some years ago. The power of remembrance
is contagious and free.

We bustle round the world,
thinking, hoping to make a difference,
and sometimes we do, because
only Him can do that.

My neighbor's language is not my own.
There are many tongues on my street:
Arabic, Swedish, Spanish, and Thai,
Nepalese, Hebrew and Chinese.

But we all walk our dogs,
whistle, feed, shampoo and love them.
Dogs and kids and old grandpas.
Only Him can do that.

THE PERUVIAN BLANKET

It's a warm thing,
woven from alpaca
or is it llama?
I know not, in truth,
but it comforts me,
as I sit in my Zen chair
with my blanket from Peru.

It speaks of love and longing,
waiting for the Godness,
the Is-ness,
the Oneness to appear.

And the silence of it all
brings gratitude for what I am,
and whom I shall become,
and especially for the gift
of my generous and gracious son.

WHAT IS THIS JOY?

What is this joy I feel?
When I sit in the morning sun,
as it pours onto my meditation chair,
I gaze in amaze at the Norfolk Pine
I love so dear.

It stands tall and straight, its omnipresence
a symbol of things in nature
that wonder me daily,
like mountains, and streams,
and the symmetry of a flower.

What is this joy I feel?
My eyes wander to the bookshelf
to ponder pics of my beloved grands,
lounging and laughing upon the sands
of a nearby beach.

Children without a care so far,
because of the wisdom and work
of parents beloved and loving,
parents I scarcely remember parenting
so carelessly myself.

What is this joy I feel?
On the piano I see remnants of travels
and times abroad and away,
tours and trips, to sing and savor
the world's flavors.

A prayer wheel from Tibet,
a Nepalese singing bowl,
an etched gourd from Peru,
a fighting bull from Spain,
and a chicken from Portugal.

What is this joy I feel?
A heart-shaped stone
from a dear, departed friend,
my mother's mis-shapen Scottie dog,
a paper-mache angel in paint of gold.

What are these things?
For they are not things at all,
not of any import, really,
except for the memories they hold,
sacred and vivid as truth.

Love expands the breast
and blooms down my arms and legs.
So many memories live here,
not in the things themselves as such,
but in my heart and soul.

Oh, I have been fortunate indeed,
and have much to be thankful for.
For what are these things, these things
that stand for the things
I love and adore?

What is this joy I feel?
Except, perhaps,
I think, maybe,
it could be nothing but
a rare good night's sleep.

HOME

There's a number of things
I don't like about home.

For one thing,
No one picks up after you,
nor washes dishes,
nor cleans the house.
Why don't clothes know the way to the hamper?
They've traveled it often enough.
And why can't books find their proper place
and dishes, the short flight to the washer?
They should be factory-trained to self-load.

But home is where my chair is,
where I sit when I want to be with you,
and my doggies come to greet me,
to wash me, to nudge and get a massage,
to nuzzle for treats in my pocket.
Ahhh…

RANDOM THOUGHTS
ABOUT DOGS

FRITZ

It wasn't far, this trip to school.
She had done it since first grade.
Three blocks from home,
what danger could lie there?

She named him Fritz when
he appeared in the yard that day.
Chiggers were biting in the grass,
but he decided to stay.

He watched as she caught fireflies
in a jar, then swung on her trapeze.
He knew she would love a furry thing,
and she did, she fell in love with ease.

When fall and school beckoned that year,
they went together, the two of them.
Out at eight o'clock, home at noon, and back at one.
Then home again at 3:15, when school was done.

They never thought what danger lurked
on Main and Seventh Street.
They waited at the lights as they had always done,
unaware of the fate they'd meet.

When the light changed, he led the way,
trotting with happy-go-lucky feet.
He had a duty to give his all
to the child he loved with every heart beat.

A semi came barreling through.
He had a quota to make.
Unaware of the precious sight,
too late, he squealed the brake.

Fritz sacrificed all.

MY DOG SHAKESPEARE (SPIER)

My dog Shakes Spier is black as coal,
except for little chest hairs,
one little white paw, and
the tiniest goatee, making him look
like the oboist in a jazz quartet, despite
an underbite and a very long tongue.

My dog Shakes Spier is stocky and strong.
A thick neck, short legs, and coiled bristle tail
work hard at hustling like a lumberjack,
as we go to the northern pines and back.
Around the block each night we go,
the walk of a mile or so.

My dog Shakes Spier is smart as a whip.
He remembers every detail
of every game and where we played it.
He's at my side all day and then some.

At night, he lies beside my heart to feel it beat.
Then when he thinks I am asleep, he retreats
to a corner, where the fan beats the heat.
If I can't sleep, he's with me, to the kitchen,
to eat and read something sleepy and deep.

"He's so ugly, he's cute," my son says
of his funny face. But he can't know
the bond between us, how full my heart
when he hops up to be scratched
and massaged, when I feel we are one,
he and I, me and him, so dear.

SAMYE

My dog Samye
waddles like a duck
when he walks.
He hiphops like a hare
when he runs,
and stalks like a jungle cat
if we pass a big dog's lair.

My dog Samye
mewls and chews his words,
like a crone with a chaw,
squeaking and vexing
til he gets to sit in my chair.

My Samye is Tibetan,
a Spaniel mixed with Papillon.
His name means Holy One
in an ancient tongue.
The lamas hired his progenitors
to nose the prayer wheel on.

After he has licked my face,
(It's important to be clean when you pray),
he sits with me as I meditate,
stretched across my fulsome lap.
Then, sated with holy thoughts,
he runs away to play.

But when the doorbell rings,
my dog Samye answers
with the song of his people,
growling and barking loud and long
to warn he is ten inches tall
and twelve pounds strong,
and he will fight to the death
to save us.

WHICH IS GREATER?

Which is greater?
A boddhisatva?
An angel?
Or a dog?

I contend it is the dog.

A dog is without judgement,
without reservation,
envy or lust.

A dog is loyal,
trusting and forgiving.
A dog loves endlessly,
and asks for nothing,

but perhaps a biscuit,
the massage of an ear,
a stroke on the belly,
as she settles into sleep

at night.

BARNEY

He was my beautiful Barney,
with long ears and freckles on his nose.
A cocker with a sense of humor, you say?
that tricks and amuses by playing a joke?
Who knows?

How I loved him, the boy with luxurious blond hair,
his perky trot and eagerness to obey.
But then, the harsh verdict one day,
a weak heart. How can he live on
this way?

But he proved the vet wrong
and lived another six months long.
His rib bones stuck out from the weight he'd lost,
but I pampered and pet him and fed him good food,
How much I love you, my Barney boy.

He died in my arms, one yelp and it was over,
mouth to mouth, even CPR,
no, there was nothing to do
to revive my Barney
except to say adieux.

And thanks for the years of cuddles and laughs,
fighting with pillow cases and hiding the ball,
and for the fun of being your friend, not boss nor keeper,
but companion on the journey of life.
I have loved it all.

RANDOM THOUGHTS
OF A CRONE

LISTEN TO YOUR PEOPLE

(written 2018, on the eve of the midterms)

Listen to the people,
hurting and hating,
confused and cornered,
battered and bruised
with the day's events.

Listen to the people,
without a clue
what to believe, what to do,
what is right or wrong
about the atrocities you do.

Listen to the people.
They know the truth
about what you say and do.
They know in their gut
which is false or true.

But you have clubbed them
into senselessness and falsity.
You have chewed them up
into an aching insanity
that has rendered them helpless.

HOW MANY DEAD TODAY?

I rise in the morning and say
"How many dead today?"
I pour a cup of coffee
and greet my sleep-tousled spouse.
"How many dead today?"

I've always been a cougher,
sinusitis the cause.
Now I cough in shame.
"Sorry, I forgot my nasal spray.
I don't have Covid, please stay."
Still, they hurry away.

How many dead today?

A cup of soup for lunch.
Keep it light to diet, but why,
when thousands die?
I read, write, cook, and play
games with my husband,
as we rage about the news of the day.

How many dead today?

I've always been a loner.
A quiet and simple life suits.
It's nice to live this way.
I like to walk the dogs, others
do the same, mumbling through masks,
"How's it going?" they say.

The birds are singing,
the sky's so blue, it's hard
to remember the gray.
Stars are out, pollution's gone.
Is climate change reversed?
But what a price to pay!

How many dead today?

My heart aches with the question,
each one a hole that cannot be filled.
How many dead today?

How many dead today?

MISSION IMPOSSIBLE

That's what they call it,
the students who try to be perfect.
They follow the Buddha,
and love without condition,
every soul, good or bad,
on track for heaven or perdition.

Namaste, they say,
looking into your eyes so deep,
they see and bless your spiritual core,
no matter your imperfection,
your thoughts, words or deeds,
murderer, thief, politician, or whore.

Namaste, I say, as I look for the good,
no matter what they say or do.
But I can harm as well as my brother.
I must judge myself as any other,
if I'm true to the life of a Boddhisatva.
It's a Mission Impossible.

THE PACKAGE DEAL

A learned person knows the answer.
A wise person knows there are many answers.
A mystic knows there are no answers at all.

Was it Buddha who taught me this?
The teacher of my agony?
No, 'twas schizophrenia,
the monster in my family's life.

The monster without purpose,
the malady without pause,
the unanswerable question -
what is its cause?

It is this misery
that taught me joy.
How should I employ
my heart without it?

So, they are gifts, really,
both misery and joy,
a dual purpose and paradox.
It's a package deal.

THE CRAWL SPACE PLACE

The crawl space place in my basement
was cold, dark, and foreboding.
It pulled and tugged whenever
I visited in my raw years.

Who would I become
if I stepped through the veil,
a new family, a new world,
a new me?

Would I dance on Fifth Street?
Eat ice cream at Rexall's?
Cross the tracks to the other side,
to the rats in the rotting old Roxy?

That strange tug on my soul,
Was it destiny? Or danger?
I don't have the tools to say.
Will I be too afraid to go some day?

Is it infinity or death that pulls me so?
When I am old and wise I will know.

THE DREAM THREE-PEATED

A maze, dusty and dim
in a desert at dawn.
Sand everywhere, floors and walls,
adobe houses clustered in a rabbit warren,
silent as stone and twice as stark.

I'm lost. How can I leave this place?
A few turbaned heads begin to wake.
"Where am I?" I ask, and "How to go elsewhere?"
Something threatens, yet no complaint I make.
This place is not for me.

Finally,
an open space, a friendly face.
The infinite beckons and I respond.
I see sand, only blowing sand.
Am I alone? Is this the way? I say.

Silence.
I am not ready, not worthy, not welcomed.
Only the wisdom I await knows.

THE REJECTED BIO

I'll use the verse
if you're not adverse,
to tell my story
in the present.

A story of grimy furniture from ungroomed dogs
in a house cluttered with a thousand books or more,
most unread, or loved and to be reread,
for the unloved are given or thrown away.

I enter most days with a gaping heart hole.
I find the world insufficient
and ignobly lacking in my estimation.
My need for truth and peace go unanswered.

Shall I worry and fuss about the dying earth?
or the hostility of a schizophrenic daughter?
They are one and the same, it seems,
her madness, an echo of Washington's bile.

Yet it is my good fortune
to have lived a life of many blessings.
A son and spouse counterbalance,
to lighten and sweeten the load.

For books and dogs and singing,
for travel, hikes, and volunteering,
for three grands of perfection,
I give profuse thanks on my knees.

For the kindness of others,
with the willingness to fight
against wrong when I cannot,
for the truth-tellers and do-gooders.

And most, I am thankful for the now,
for the beauty of a flower,
the billowing cloud in the sky,
the warp and woof of the bark on that tree

that smiles at me when we go walking by.
And for you, whoever you are,
that reads this page just now.
I am thankful for you, too.

RANDOM THOUGHTS
WITH A LIGHT TOUCH

EYES OR EARS

It's a childish game, for sure,
played when but a tween,
lying on the grass with the chiggers,
and a buddy from far-away years.

Ears are cool, without them,
there'd be no Brahms,
Britten, Bach, or Beethoven.
Even then I had good taste.

There'd be no rustling in the breeze
on a trail through windy trees,
where the brook babbles and gargles,
no snap of a twig to bring alarm.

Yet the memory of these is so poignant,
even if the hearing is replaced forever
by feeling, by seeing, by tasting, and smelling,
I should not regret nor complain.

If I were to lose my eyes, however,
lose the delight of all those sights,
the expanse of sky, the depth
and hue of the deep blue sea.

I'd lose my books, even the poetry,
for I've never been one to memorize.
I'd sooner cut off a toe than lose
a Mary Oliver, Rilke or Rumi.

So my answer is final,
I say, quite unequivocably,
if I have to choose to lose,
it'll be the ears for me.

ODE TO MY DUODENUM

My stalwart companion for a million meals,
you've put up with sugary cobblers and greasy grits,
spicy grasshoppers and chicken feet,
never complaining, never ceasing
to devour and conquer what I assign.
Your quiet presence belies your importance
to my digestive design.

What have you not conquered?
Yet where are your laurels?
Is your gravestone to be void
of accolades and compliments?
Shall you never be awarded the promise
of rest and retirement after a job well done,
you good and faithful servant?

Maybe you are the God core of our being,
the essence to whom we give homage,
when all else is said and done and we are freed.
For without you, our favorite pastime is gone,
not baseball, nor shopping, nor even walking,
but the one thing that makes us one,
one for all and all for one –
eating!

MY MO-JO

I got my mo-jo back!
I'm not sure what that means,
But for me, mo-jo is more joy!

Holidays are hard.
Plenty of reminders about what is wrong,
memories, regrets and no control
over what brings the joy.

Do you feel me?

It can be hard to do the good things,
even the things you enjoy.
Grand parties and parties with grands,
difficult relations, pressure for presents,
superfluous gifts that disappoint and bore.

So I cheer for routine,
Even though it may surprise.
My mo-jo comes with the old things.
It just arrives.

I CHOOSE JOY WITH GRITTED TEETH

It's hard to get up in the morning.
The bed is warm, eyes closed,
brain unaware of the cares
of the world which is
distant and vague.

But then, the effort to put a foot down
hurts to the core, every step a new ache.
The weather's fowl, the news disgusting,
and the world is doomed,
a bleak and unendurable place.

I don't have anything against mornings.
On paper, they are quite acceptable,
a time for rosy skies and crisp air,
a time of dewy grass, and singing birds,
a time of hope, new starts and crumb cake.

But sometimes, I can scarce breathe
with the worries – physical and emotional –
that burden my soul.
Why should I live another minute?
I ask myself rhetorically.

I have the answer, of course,
My very good fortune, of course,
family and friends, of course,
music and art, travel and books,
and don't forget the dogs, of course.

Especially, don't forget the dogs,
as they rush to greet me.
I can judge completely
how much they need me,
as their slippery tongues lick my face.

So mornings are not definitive
of the warp and woof of my day.
I know the time-worn remedies:
coffee, meditation, a reading of sorts,
and most, a heaping tablespoon of gratitude,

Yes, a tablespoon of gratitude
is good for your attitude, they say.
Then I can greet the day
and my joy with gritted teeth.
All things will be better by noon.

REFLECTION

In the end
I was no wise man,
no missionary that trudged the desert sands,
nor survived the treacherous seas.
But I could give a hug.

In the end
I was no famous singer,
nor teacher inspiring students to lead,
nor critic of film, books, and performances.
But I could give a hug.

My soul cries out for a cushioned meeting
of my heart with another, breast to breast,
I long for the warmth that makes us one,
But Covid stole my purpose away.

In the end
I was no doctor that heals and saves,
no cop, nor fireman, nor social worker
that helps, aids, and rescues those in need.
But I could give a hug, the only gift I had,
Til Covid took it away.

AN APOLOGY TO KONDO

My house is a clutter
and I like it that way,
Offend others? It may.
It's abominable, Marie would say.

There are books all 'round
and dog-made grime.
I cover it all with afghans,
but it's not a crime.

I know where my things are,
my 200 must read and re-read books.
my guilty pleasure, you might say.
I'll get to them some day.

There's one other apology to make
to my children and grand-children, I think.
They may learn to hate the stuff I love,
when I pass at 108.

IS IT SOUP YET?

Soup's on!

Leftovers loom and threaten
in the back of the refrigerator.
What mystery meat dares to lead the charge?
A quartet of the familiar dependables:
celery, garlic, carrots, and onions,
seasoned soldiers of my culinary battles,
led by General Bouillon
of Chicken or Beef battalions.
Metaphors marry like musty flavors:
broccoli and beans, battle-scarred and tipsy,
a splash of wine, an hour or two,
a delicate sip from the soup scoop.

Magic happens!

RANDOM THOUGHTS
ON PURPOSE

REFLECTIONS BEFORE SURGERY

I am a deeply flawed person.
I've done a lot of stuff in my life,
a life not useful particularly,
except I've given a hug or three.

I am a deeply flawed person.
I've traveled to 42 countries,
seen mountains and oceans,
and the mystery of a tree,
and I've given a hug or three.

I am a deeply flawed person.
I've taught a few souls a two or thing,
but never invented, nor cured a disease,
nor saved a life in all its ecstasy,
but I've given a hug or three.

I am a deeply flawed person.
I've sung many a song,
recitals, even an opera or three.
I've known the joy of perfect harmony,
and I've given a hug or three.

I'm a deeply flawed person.
I've basked in the sun,
counted the tunes of a mockingbird,
and studied the veins of a leaf,
and I've given a hug or three.

I'm a deeply flawed person,
blessed, nevertheless, by family and friends.
I've known their undeserved love
through good times and bad,
so I've given a hug or three.

I'm a deeply flawed person.
I've read a thousand books,
searched for God and meaning,
and found the courage to die free,
because I've given a hug or three.

I'm a deeply flawed person.
I've done a lot of stuff in my life,
a life not useful particularly,
except I've given a hug or three.

LOVE IS A MUSCLE,
USE IT OR LOSE IT

It occurs to me, the opposite of love
Is not hate, but separation.
We are meant to be One, I think,
when I perceive the tenuous threads
and gauzy links of living.
And the Oneness is to breathe
the universe that gives us life.

I ask forgiveness
for an insensitive youth,
for the slowness of learning life's lessons.
I ask forgiveness for the distraction
of the moneyed world,
for it is a sin not to know or care
that we are love on a journey.

A journey to love,
and to know there is no journey,
for we are already home.
A journey to love oneself,
then to discard, for what are we,
except God in a body?
Letting go of that, we are free,
free to love the world.

WHAT DO YOU SEE?

If you see an insane world,
the world will be insane.

If you judge the world,
the world will be condemned.

If you forgive the world,
the world will be merciful and kind.

THE JOURNEY

We are on a journey, you and I.
It is a journey home.
It's not important where we've been,
or where we may have yet to go,
but only that we journey on,
beckoned by God alone.

Some want to be with another,
a duet of sorts, marching two by two.
Others need a crowd of admirers,
friends and family galore,
a virtual city traveling together,
a congratulatory clamor of hugs to explore.

Occasionally, there's a solitary sort,
by choice or fate, I know not,
but I feel the weight of their loneliness.
Unrequited love, perhaps, or the loss of hope
from years gone by. Namaste, I say
with fervent intention and silent prayer.

As for myself, I need the silence of time
to reflect and grow, to open my heart and mind,
to feel the love that pours like gold
into the hole of duality split in two.
The presence of God fills me up,
but the fullness of friends and loved ones
spills over all, balancing the gifts of both.
Life is a journey, in purpose and truth.

Which choice is best, you ask?
Which feeds the other?
Ah, I cannot answer.
It is your question, your conundrum.

It is a lifelong quest,
a journey that is yours alone.
But I am here with you
to give you what love I can.

PARADOX

I believe this.
I also believe that.
This and that.
That and this.
They cancel each other,
yet both are true.

How can that be?
It's not negation,
but co-habitation.
They are one and the same.
One makes possible
the other's creation.

All things are One.
It is this that describes
our wholeness,
our Oneness, and
if we are true to ourselves,
our little bit of holiness.

THE CHRISTMAS TREE

It's almost March and still –
the Christmas tree awaits,
gracing my living room
for the third month.

Why? You say? The needles drop,
the branches droop, the balls fall off.
Not even the dog wants to fetch any more.
It looks wan and weary.

No, it's artificial, I say.
Purchased second hand from the Daze,
The best fake I've seen.
Lingering in front of the slider.

And blocking the view of my favorite tree –
the Norfolk Pine – which helps me to center,
in my worn-out chair, to meditate,
and feel the warmth of memories.

The home-made decorations
of four generations, the gifts of kith
and kin, and the treasured mementos
from trips abroad.

I see a plaster angel,
made by my artistic sister,
with an O-shaped mouth, singing
as I do, of the reason for the season.

There are many angels, in fact,
from Mexico, Hungary, and Peru.
There is one of fake pearls, fashioned
by my Mom before she passed.

Many Santas, of course, my favorite
is sloppily and hastily painted,
from one of the grands, I suppose,
I forget which one.

There's an ice-skating Santa,
and another playing golf.
An angel lounges in a champagne flute.
Those friends knew us only too well.

A picture of my daughter from early days,
in a frame sewn of red and white checks
A long-gone baby-sitter's doing, perhaps?
During some long-gone Ohio night, I reflect?

The requisite bird-in-nest close to the trunk,
a tradition from David's Mom, now mourned,
and a tiny creche from a nephew
when my first grandchild was born.

There are many gifts nestled in the tree,
from gift exchanges of one or another,
a P.E.O. chapter, or in days gone by,
co-workers and dear departed friends.

The old Smithsonian angel at the top
was our first collaborative purchase.
Thoughtlessly packed with red candles,
her lacy dress, a melted pink.

Stiff stains on her voluminous skirt
remind us the beauty of our mistakes molds
and makes us into the gentle forgiving folk
we need to be.

So, I'm keeping the tree for awhile,
to count and catalogue its lessons.
Memories too numerous to list here
of those forgotten, yet loved as well.

I need not be reminded
as I reminisce beside this visual aid,
how grateful I am
for a blest and bountiful life.

A LEGACY OF LOVE

Twenty-five years goes by in a flash
One blink and it is gone.
Lost in the rubble of diapers and dreams,
Of soccer balls, basketballs, and fundraising schemes.
Gone are birthday streamers and Shutterfly trips,
Prom gowns, mortar boards, and driving tests.
Suddenly, you are alone, you two,
In a mansion echoing with memories.

Sometimes it must have seemed too hard,
Too many Herculean tasks to complete,
Too many personalities to mold and shape
Into more malleable futures, and better fates,
Did the two of you always see eye to eye?
Were you in harmony on the journey
Of magic and mystery?

In the end, it hardly matters.
The marriage goes on, but the job is done.
Your joint triple creation of life and limb
Could not be more perfect
As it proves your legacy of love.

RANDOM THOUGHTS
OF GOD

WHAT (WHO) IS GOD?

The Universe looming,
all of nature crackling,
from the tiny ladybug
to the towering moss-covered oak,
this is the God I love.

As for the father's arm outstretched,
finger pointing,
eyes cast down,
too overbearing for my taste,
I prefer a he/she/it sort of thing
to create.

But late at night as I lie awake,
waiting for the Ambien to kick in,
I remember my brother Yeshua,
and ask him what he makes
of the regrets of my day.

Is there a betrayal in this paradox?
I think not.

GRACE

"There but for the grace of God, go I."
That's what my mother said,
passing a beggar on the street,
or some other unfortunate soul.

She was always careful
to use the appropriate tense.
The schoolteacher would say,
"I, not me, is correct in this case."

My older siblings told stories, however,
about the Depression and the dust bowl years
in Oklahoma, that made me wonder,
had she always known the "grace of God"?

And what was the grace of God anyway?
It's a question I've posed for years.
Even Billy Graham confused me once.
Why do we need grace to save?

And what is saved anyway?
Saved from what? Or who?
From no grace? From the place
on the street where the beggar lay?

Or is it lies? Or lain?
I can't ask my mother.
She's gone now,
saved from the beggar's fate.

I assume she knows though,
having gone past wisdom
to the No-thing of the beyond.
She knew even before, I suspect.

She called me to her wheelchair
at the last, or soon to be,
taking my hand, eyes closed,
voice in a husky whisper.

"You were right," she rasped.
"Reincarnation is," referring
to an old battle in my youth.
"I see it now."

Was it the morphine talking?
Or the God-force she met
on her way to journey's end?
to what she wanted to be?

Decades have gone by,
years of pain and joy.
Yet still I wonder
What is grace?

I'm an old crone myself
and know a thing or three.
I know that for me, at least,
Grace is simply to be.

To know God's love
or whoever, I don't care.
Perhaps a force, or a No-thing,
but a Oneness is my prayer.

The willingness to accept the love
whenever and wherever it comes,
not believing in it, as Billy would say,
but knowing it in heart and soul.

THE DISCO BALL THEORY

It's a metaphor I can understand,
for its universe, scope, and purpose.
I imagine a great disco ball
dangling from the ceiling of infinity,
twisting in the light, each piece twinkling,
a tiny mirror reflecting, inviting new delight.

It invites us in, and down the slide
to another culture, another place and life.
Each piece is a thought: Islam, Hindu, Sufi or Juda,
Christian, Tao, Shinto and Buddha, each
beckoning to another world, another way.

The more we go down the tunnel,
the more we read, talk, think, and see,
the more it's all the same.
It's the mystical center that unites us,
and makes us One.

MY GOOD FRIEND YESHUA

My good friend Yeshua
(sometimes I call him Josh)
is the perfect listener
when I feel sad or lost.

Sometimes I tell him things
I'd rather not tell anyone,
things of shame or jealousy,
or guilt for a thing not done.

Then my mind goes elsewhere
off to Metamusil and mindcraft,
to laundry and longings
for unknown journeys and whatnot.

Even if thanks are remembered,
and prayers for those in need,
where the brain will wander
is an astonishing thing indeed.

My good friend Yeshua
(sometimes I call him Josh)
Others call him Jesus,
but I care not.

SOMETIMES

Sometimes my friend Yeshua
comes home from wars in Washington,
battered and bruised, but
nevertheless, hopeful.

I want to bandage his brokenness,
the cut above his eye, his aching ribs,
for he took a body blow
of hypocrisy and hate.

But he takes me into his arms
and asks about me.
How was my day?
Did your work go okay?

And it is I who cries.

Why should my small concerns
(for they are small indeed)
take precedence over his big ones?
My question spills out with a need to know.

My fears, regrets and longings
Are but an afterthought, I think,
when all is said and done,
when I contemplate his bigger ones.

The earth is dying, I think to myself,
and our country's democracy with it.
The goodness of humankind is battling
for survival, along with decency and kindness.

You can find these anachronisms
in the streets of Anytown,
but even the basics
are absent in the halls of power.

So why should my small self matter?
My anger for a stubbed toe,
or the slight of an unexpected truth-telling
by someone's frustration with my wayward ways?

Because you are loved, my dear.
You are the world to me, right now,
and in every now, he says, as he kisses
my brow and wisps through my mind.

And it is I who cries.

THE HOLINESS OF
THE WHOLENESS

As I sit in silence to contemplate
the holiness of the wholeness,
peace comes.

As I sit in peace to contemplate
the holiness of the wholeness,
love comes.

As I sit with love to contemplate
the holiness of the wholeness,
joy comes.

As I sit in joy to contemplate
the holiness of the wholeness,
understanding comes.

As I sit with understanding to contemplate
the holiness of the wholeness,
the no-thing comes.

And then I know
the wholeness of the holiness,
and I am home.

THE BREAD AND THE WINE

Nibble and sip,
Nibble and sip.
I kneel at the rail
and await the Godness.

Nibble and sip,
Nibble and sip.
I pray the wounded world to be
healed and whole.

Nibble and sip,
Nibble and sip.
She comes to fill me, to make me
healed and whole.

Nibble and sip,
Nibble and sip.
The Godness of All speaks
and brings peace.

HOLD ME

(inspired by Mike Kinman's Christmas Eve sermon)

Will I be safe?
Will I be happy?
Will I be loved?

Hold me, hold me, hold me,
the newborn silently screams
to the womb so recently
vanished.

The cry consumes us all,
the cry that binds us,
the cry that makes us human,
the cry that brings us together.

We need to be touched,
our fingertips, our lips.
The stories of our bodies
are the timetables of touch.

We are a fearful people,
vulnerable and restless in our faith,
if the touch does not come,
if it brings betrayal, hurt, and hate.

We crave the touch.
We need the touch,
the touch of the other
that makes us whole.

Hold me, hold me, hold me.
Christmas is the song of longing for touch.
Christmas is our story,
our timetable of touch,
God's touch, our touch.

ANTHEM

I don't believe in God.
I know God.
In many ways I try not to.
I say "there is no proof".
I ask questions galore,
and don't wait for the truth.
"I have stuff to do," I say.

But then I find God
as I walk down the street.
God's the tree-maker,
the flower painter,
the imaginer of furry forms
that lead their two-legged friends
by the leash.

I breathe
and God is there,
the inventor of a multitude
of masks we wear,
cultures with tiny tracks
of tribe and tradition.
Where does what is you stop
and what is me begin?

Eat up the fences that divide us.
Smudge out the borders
of nation and creed,
of power and greed.
Shout out far and wide
God is One
God is Us.

Let the rivers and rodents
join in the chorus.
Inhabitor of every house and home.
never mind how great or small,
shout out to one and all.
God is One.
God is Us.

CPSIA information can be obtained
at www.ICGtesting.com
Printed in the USA
BVHW031830080422
633814BV00013B/64